This copy of
THE
HAUNTED HOUSE
JOKE BOOK
belongs to:~
ROBBIE L.

THE HAUNTED HOUSE JOKE BOOK

John Hegarty

Illustrated by Jean Baylis

Red Fox Books

A Red Fox Book
Published by Arrow Books Limited
20 Vauxhall Bridge Road, London SW1V 2SA

An imprint of the Random Century Group Ltd

London Melbourne Sydney Auckland
Johannesburg and agencies throughout the world

First published 1990

Set in Century Schoolbook
by JH Graphics Ltd, Reading

Made and printed in Great Britain
by Courier International Ltd
Tiptree, Essex

ISBN 0 09 962150 9

Contents

Spooky spectres in the sitting-room

What do women ghosts who have been in hospital love to do?
Talk about their apparitions.

FIRST GHOST: You look tried.
SECOND GHOST: Yes, I'm dead on my feet.

Where do ghost trains stop?
At a manifestation.

What motto do ghosts hate?
'Never say die'.

Why did the girl marry the ghost?
She didn't know what possessed her.

A man's car broke down on a cold and wind-swept night, near an eerie-looking castle in Transylvania. The wizened old butler there invited the man to stay the night, and showed him to his room. It was dark and spooky, and the man was scared. 'I hope you'll be comfortable,' said the butler. 'But if you need anything during the night, just scream . . .'

What did the girl ghost do for a living?
She was a gone-gone dancer.

What do little ghosts play with?
Deady bears.

FIRST GHOUL: Do ghosts like the dead?
SECOND GHOUL: Of corpse they do!

What do you get if you leave bones out in the sun?
A skeletan.

FIRST GHOST: I want a ghoul friend.
SECOND GHOST: All right then, I'll see what I can dig up.

Why would nobody visit the posh ghost?
Because he had such a ghastly manor.

Where do ghosts go to church?
Westmonster Abbey.

When do ghosts haunt skyscrapers?
When they are in high spirits.

A headless ghost went to the Lost Property Department. The man behind the desk looked up and said: 'Sorry mate, I can't help you. You need Head Office . . .'

What weighed 20 stone and haunted Paris?
The Fat-tum of the Opera.

What did the doctor say to the ghost's wife?
'I can't see anything wrong with your husband.'

When do ghosts have to stop scaring people?
When they lose their haunting licences.

'Who's that at the door?'
'It's a ghost, dear.'
'Tell him I can't see him.'

Sign in front of a cemetery:
DUE TO A STRIKE, GRAVEDIGGING WILL BE DONE
BY A SKELETON CREW.

What did one ghost prisoner say to the other ghost prisoner?
'If we had the guts, we'd get out of here.'

Knock, Knock.
Who's there?
Boo.
Boo who?
I'm only a ghost, there's no need to cry about it . . .

What do ghosts think about parties?
The morgue the merrier.

Where do ghosts go for seaside holidays?
Goole.

Why did the ghost buy his wife a girdle for Christmas?
So that she could keep her ghoulish figure.

What is the scariest fairy tale?
Ghouldilocks and the Three Brrrrs.

How do we know that 'S' is a scary letter?
Because it makes cream scream.

What's the quickest way to escape from a ghost?
Run!

How do ghosts travel?
On fright trains.

Who is in charge of a haunted police station?
The inspectre.

Which musician do ghosts like best?
James Ghoulway.

What is the ghosts' favourite Yuletide song?
I'm Dreaming of a Fright Christmas.

What do you call the spot in the middle of a
graveyard?
The dead centre.

Who did the ghost marry?
His ghoul-friend.

What is a skeleton's favourite pop group?
Boney M.

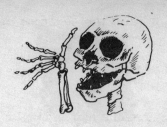

What did the skeleton say to his friend?
'I've got a bone to pick with you.'

What do you get if you cross a skeleton with a famous detective?
Sherlock Bones.

Booo-ks from the ghost library:

The Omen by B. Warned
Horror Story by Denise R. Knockin
Boo! by Terry Fie
Poltergeists by Eve L. Spirit
Ghosts and Ghoulies by Sue Pernatural

Which ghost was President of France?
Charles de Ghoul.

Did you hear about the doctor who crossed a parrot with a ghost?
It bit his arm off and said: 'Who's a pretty boy then?'

What do you call a skeleton that never does any work?
Lazy bones.

What do you get if you cross a ghost with a packet of crisps?
Snacks that go crunch in the night.

Which musical instrument does a skeleton play?
A trom-bone.

What does a ghost call its parents?
Mum and Dead.

What do ghosts eat?
Dread and butter pudding.

What sort of violin does a musical ghost play?
A dreadivarius.

What's the first thing a ghost does when it gets into the front seat of a car?
Fasten the sheet belt.

How do ghosts learn songs?
They read the sheet music.

Where do ghost trains cross roads?
At devil crossings.

Scary skeletons in the scullery

What did the teacher ghost say to the lazy pupil ghosts?
You don't seem to have any school spirit any more!

What position does a ghost play in a football team?
Ghoulie.

Why are cemeteries so popular?
Who knows, but people are dying to get into them!

Why did the ghost go into hospital?
To have his ghoul-stones removed.

How do ghosts like their eggs?
Terror-fried!

What is the little ghosts' favourite TV show?
Strange Hill.

Where do ghosts send their laundry?
To the dry screamers.

At which weight do ghosts box?
Phantom weight.

What do ghosts sing at football matches?
Here we ghost, here we ghost, here we ghost . . .

Why didn't the spook like to join in the athletic contest?
He knew he didn't have a ghost of a chance of winning.

How did skeletons send each other letters in the days of the wild west?
By Bony Express!

How long did the ghost plan to stay in London?
Not long — he was just passing through.

Why do ghosts hate rain?
It dampens their spirits.

What flowers do ghosts like growing?
Mari-ghouls and morning gorys.

What do you call a pretty ghost?
Boootiful.

How do you make a skeleton laugh?
Easy — just tickle his funny bone.

What is a skeleton?
Someone who went on a diet and forgot to say 'when'

Did you hear about the skeleton that was attacked by a dog?
It ran off with some bones and left him without a leg to stand on.

Why are skeletons usually so calm?
Nothing gets under their skin.

What weighs a thousand kilogrammes but is all bone?
A skele-tonne.

What is a ghost child's favourite bedtime story?
Ghouldilocks and the Three Pall-bearers.

Did you hear about the ghost who listened to too many stories about humans and scared himself half to life?

What do you call a skeleton who's always telling lies?
A bony phony.

What did the skeleton say to his friend?
'I've got a bone to pick with you.'

What do you get if you cross a skeleton with a famous detective?
Sherlock Bones.

Young ghosts should be heard — not seen!

What's top of the ghost pop charts?
'What Kind of Ghoul am I?'

What do you call a really professional ghost?
Deadicated.

What's even more invisible than a ghost?
A ghost's shadow.

In which book do the names of ghosts appear?
Boo's Who!

People keep canaries and parrots as pets. What do ghosts keep?
Boo-jies.

What kind of dog does a ghost have?
A boo-dle.

How can you tell when a ghost is about to faint?
It turns as white as a sheet.

What is the favourite game of ghost children?
Peekaboooo.

When ghosts need medicine, which chemist's do they go to?
Boooots.

What do you call a stupid skeleton?
A numbskull.

What is the scariest letter?
'G' because it turns a host into a ghost!

What do ghosts eat for breakfast?
Shrouded wheat.

Why do ghosts travel in lifts?
To raise their spirits.

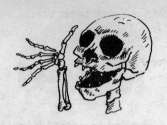

What do spooks love to drink?
Tomb-ato juice.

Did you hear about the ghost comedian?
He was booed off the stage.

Did you hear about the headless ghost that got a
job in a department store?
He's the head buyer.

What do you call a ghost that stays out all night?
A fresh-air freak.

Did you hear about the ghosts' party?
They had a wail of a time.

Where do ghosts pick up their mail?
At a dead-letter box.

How does a ghost count?
One, BOO, three, four, five, six, seven, HATE, nine, frighTEN.

What do you call a female ghost who is very fat?
A ghostess with the mostess.

What happened to the author who died?
He became a ghost writer.

What did the hippie ghost say to his girlfriend?
'Hey girl, you're really out of sight!'

Why did the two ghosts go to see the horror film?
Because they loved each shudder.

The ghoul stood on the bridge one night,
Its lips were all a-quiver;
It gave a cough,
Its leg fell off,
And floated down the river.

What do you find in a haunted cellar?
Whines and spirits.

How do skeletons communicate with each other?
They use the tele-bone.

Devilish demons in the dungeon

What do you call ghost children?
Boys and ghouls.

Which skeleton was once Emperor of France?
Napoleon Bone-apart.

What did one ghost say to the other?
'It's nice not to see you again.'

How do ghosts begin a letter?
'Tomb it may concern . . .'

What kind of plate does a skeleton eat off?
Bone china.

FIRST GHOST: I've just bought a haunted bicycle.
SECOND GHOST: How do you know it's haunted?
FIRST GHOST: There are spooks in the wheels.

Who appears on the cover of horror magazines?
The cover ghouls!

What did the estate agent say to the ghost?
'I'm sorry, sir, we have nothing suitable for haunting at the moment.'

What is big, invisible, has four wheels and flies?
The ghost town dustcart.

Why do ghosts like living in tall buildings?
Because they have lots of scarecases.

What's the best way of warding off ghostly doctors?
Always carry an apple with you.

Why did Nelson's ghost wear a three-cornered hat?
To keep his head warm.

BABY GHOST: How does it feel to hurtle through
  doors and walls?
GROWN-UP GHOST: It hurtles.

Did you hear about the little ghost who couldn't
sleep at night?
His brother kept telling him human stories.

FIRST GHOST: I hear you've got a new job.
SECOND GHOST: Yes, I'm working for a spiritualist.
FIRST GHOST: Is he any good?
SECOND GHOST: Oh, medium, I'd say.

FIRST GHOST: I went to the graveyard today.
SECOND GHOST: Someone dead?
FIRST GHOST: Yes, all of them.

What's the difference between a vampire with toothache and a rainstorm?
One roars with pain and the other pours with rain.

What is Dracula's favourite breed of dog?
The bloodhound.

What is red, sweet, and bites people in the neck?
A jampire.

Who is a vampire likely to fall in love with?
The girl necks door.

Why is Dracula a good person to take out to dinner?
Because he eats necks to nothing.

Did you hear about the skeleton that was attacked by a dog?
It ran off with some bones and left him without a leg to stand on.

What do you call a duck with fangs?
Count Quackula.

BABY GHOST: Mummy, mummy, am I a real ghost?
MOTHER GHOST: Of course you are.
BABY GHOST: Are you absolutely sure?
MOTHER GHOST: Of course I'm sure. Why do you ask?
BABY GHOST: Because I hate the dark!

Which disease do ghosts fear the most?
The boo-bonic plague.

Did you hear about the two unmarried ghosts who lived together?
They believed in doing what comes supernaturally.

Where does a ghost keep his car?
In the mirage.

'Do you believe in ghosts?'
'*Of course not.*'
Would you spend the night in a haunted house then?'
'*No.*'
'Whyever not?'
'*I might be wrong.*'

29

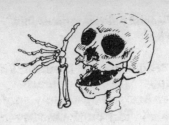

FIRST GHOST: Where did you go for your holiday?
SECOND GHOST: The Savoy hotel.
FIRST GHOST: The Savoy? That's one of my favourite haunts.

Did you hear about the group of ghosts who got together to protest against air pollution?
They held a haunt-in in front of the Houses of Parliament.

What sort of society do vampires join?
A blood group.

What frozen food company is run by Dracula?
Fiendus Foods.

Why was Dracula lost on the motorway?
He was looking for the main artery.

What do you get if you cross a vampire with a car?
A monster that attacks vehicles and sucks out all their petrol.

What is a vampire's favourite animal?
The giraffe (just think of all that neck!)

Why should vampires never be trusted?
Because they are fly-by-nights.

Did you hear about the new vampire doll?
You wind it up and it bites Barbie on the neck.

What do you get if you cross a vampire with Al Capone?
A fangster!

A mother ghost brought her child to the doctor. 'Please see what's wrong with him.' she said. 'He's always in such good spirits.'

A woman went up to a ghost and said: 'How much would you charge to give my husband a good fright?' 'For £10,' replied the ghost, 'I'll scare him out of his wits.' 'Good,' said the woman. 'Here's £5 – he's only a half wit!'

What kind of a spook can you hold on the end of your finger?
A bogey

Did you hear about the ghost that ate the Christmas decorations?
He died of tinselitis.

There once was a ghost from Darjeeling,
Who got on a train bound for Ealing;
It said at the door,
'Please don't sit on the floor' –
So he floated up and sat on the ceiling.

Where do ghosts go to live when they retire?
Gravesend.

What's white, very sleekly built, and beats all other spooks from a standing start?
A turbo-charged phantom.

Lady Jane Grey
Had nothing to say.
What could she have said
After losing her head?

What is a skeleton?
Someone who went on a diet and forgot to say 'when'.

What does a ghost look like?
Like nothing you've ever seen before.

What do you call a school for female ghosts?
An all-ghouls school.

Ghastly ghouls in the gallery

Why do demons and ghouls get on so well?
Because demons are a ghoul's best friend.

Which ghost made friends with the three bears?
Ghouldilocks.

Why couldn't the skeleton go to the ball?
Because he had no body to go with.

Where do ghosts stay when they go on holiday?
At a ghost-house.

FIRST GHOST: I don't seem to frighten people any more.
SECOND GHOST: I know. We might as well be dead for all they care.

FIRST GHOST: I find haunting castles really boring
these days.
SECOND GHOST: I know what you mean. I don't just
seem able to put any life into it.

What happens when a ghost retires?
He receives a ghoulden handshake.

Why do skeletons drink milk?
Because it's good for the bones.

How do ghost doctors prevent diseases in young
ghost children?
They give them boooster shots!

What do ghosts wear in the rain?
Boo-ts and ghoul-oshes.

Why are skeletons usually so calm?
Nothing gets under their skin.

What kind of dates do ghosts go out with?
Anyone they can dig up.

What famous play about ghosts was written by
William Shakespeare?
Romeo and Ghouliet.

What do you call a swarm of ghost bees?
Zombees.

How do you make a skeleton laugh?
Easy — just tickle his funny bone.

What ghost was a famous explorer?
Christopher Ghoulumbus.

What weighs 1000 kilogrammes but is all bone?
A skele-tonne.

What do you call a skeleton who's always telling lies?
A bony phony.

'Where shall I meet you?' asked the ghost boy to the ghost girl. 'Under the clothes line,' she said; 'that's where I hang out!'

Sign in front of a cemetery: **DUE TO A STRIKE, GRAVEDIGGING WILL BE DONE BY A SKELETON CREW**.

What do you call a stupid skeleton?
A numbskull.

How did skeletons send each other letters in the days of the wild west?
By Bony Express!

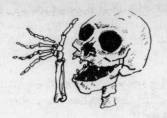

What did the old skeleton complain of?
Aching bones!

What's yellow with fangs and webbed feet?
Count Duckula.

Why did Dracula always carry his coffin with him?
His life was at stake.

What do you think the tiniest vampire in the world gets up to at night?
Your ankles.

Four ghosts were playing cards when a fifth ghost opened the door and came in. It was windy outside, and all the cards were blown off the table. One of the ghost players was very annoyed. 'For goodness sake,' he said, 'why don't you come in through the keyhole like everyone else?'

Did you hear about the ghost who went to the barber's for a haircut? 'I'm busy,' said the barber. 'You'll have to wait.' 'That's all right,' said the ghost. 'I'll leave my head here and call back for it later.'

What's white and scary and hides in corners?
An embarrassed ghost.

How should you address the Lord High Ghost?
Your Ghostliness.
And how should you address the Lord High Ghoul?
Your Ghastliness.

What does a female ghost throw to the bridesmaids at her wedding?
Her boooquet!

Why wasn't the ghost very popular with girls at parties?
He wasn't much to look at.

Why is a haunted house like a rabbit farm?
They're both hair- (hare-) raising places.

What happened when the ghost went to the theatre?
All the actors got stage fright.

What is a ghost's favourite song?
Oh What a Beautiful Mourning.

Where do cowboy ghosts live?
In a ghost town.

Why don't ghosts make good magicians?
You can see right through their tricks.

What's the best way of avoiding infection from biting ghosts?
Don't bite any ghosts.

FIRST GHOST: We've found a really nice hotel for our holidays.
SECOND GHOST: A real home from home, is it?
FIRST GHOST: Oh yes, they don't change the sheets from one year to the next.

There was once a bald ghost-hunter who went to spend the night in a haunted house. After dinner he went up the eerie staircase to the spooky bedroom, where someone had once reported seeing a terrifying ghost. He put on his pyjamas, cleaned his teeth, climbed into bed, and took off the black wig that he always wore and hung it on the bedpost. Then he settled down to wait for the ghost to arrive. By midnight, however, nothing had happened, and he dropped off to sleep.

'Some haunted house,' he said to himself the next morning. 'What a waste of time; mind you I haven't slept so well for years.' As he spoke he reached out for his wig on the bedpost. He was just about to put it on when he realized that something wasn't quite right. The wig had turned totally white . . .

A ghost was out haunting one night when it came across a fairy prancing around the forest. 'Hello,' said the ghost. 'I've never met a fairy before. What's your name?' 'Nuff,' said the fairy. 'That's a very odd name,' replied the ghost. 'No it's not,' said the fairy. 'Haven't you heard of Fairy Nuff?'

The lady ghost went to buy some new clothes at Phantom Phashions, the spooky bootique. 'I'd like to try on that shroud in the window,' she said to the assistant. 'Yes, madam,' said the assistant, 'but wouldn't you prefer to use the changing room?'

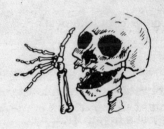

Gruesome gremlins in the garden

What do baby ghosts like chewing?
Boo-ble gum.

What trees do ghosts like best?
Ceme-trees.

What is the best way for a ghost-hunter to keep fit?
Exorcise regularly.

What is a ghost's favourite music?
Haunting melodies.

What do you call twin ghosts who keep ringing doorbells?
Dead ringers.

What game do ghosts like to play at parties?
Haunt and seek.

What does a ghost take for a bad cold?
Coffin drops.

What do you get if you cross a witch with a werewolf?
A mad dog that chases aeroplanes.

What do you get if you cross a hairdresser with a werewolf?
A monster with an all-over perm.

'Mummy, Mummy, what's a werewolf?'
'Shut up, and comb your face.'

What happened to the wolf that fell into the washing machine?
It became a wash and werewolf.

Who puts the ghosts' point of view at their press conference?
A spooksman.

What do ghosts buy to put in their coffee?
Evaporated milk.

What do you do with a green ghost?
Wait until he's ripe.

FIRST GHOST: How did you get that terrible bump on your head?
SECOND GHOST: I was floating through a keyhole when some idiot put the key in the lock.

What do you get if you cross a ghost with an official on a train?
A ticket inspectre.

What happened to the man who refused to pay his exorcist's bill?
He was repossessed.

What happened when the ghostly cows got out of their field?
There was udder chaos.

There once was a young ghost from Gloucester,
Whose parents imagined they'd lost her;
From the fridge came a sound,
And at last she was found,
But the problem was how to defrost her.

What was the ghostly medical student's first job?
Going around scaring people out of their hiccoughs.

Why did the ghost go into the chemist's?
To collect his film transparencies.

Which ghost sailed the seven seas looking for rubbish and blubber?
The ghost of Binbag the Whaler.

What should you do if you find that your bedroom is haunted?
Move house.

What did the camper feel when he realized that his sleeping bag was haunted?
Intense (in tents) fear.

Why was the headless ghost sent to the mental hospital?
Because he wasn't all there.

What is the name of the nervous ghost who rides through the desert?
The Shake of Araby.

What happened when the phantom cavalier lost his head?
He sent for a head hunter.

How can you tell if a ghost is a member of CND?
He goes on demon-strations.

Did you hear about the spook who went on the F-plan diet?
He had beans on ghost twice a day.

Who do ghosts call in if they don't feel too well?
The surgical spirit.

FIRST GHOST: You can tell I'm getting old – I'm supposed to be invisible but I'm beginning to show.

SECOND GHOST: Then I've got just the thing for you – vanishing cream.

BABY GHOST: Mummy, mummy, tell me another story about the haunted house.

MOTHER GHOST: I can't darling, it's a one-storey building.

What is the final dance at the ghosts' ball?
The last vaults.

FIRST GHOST: I've decided to hang up my shroud and go and join the land of the living.

SECOND GHOST: You haven't?

FIRST GHOST: No, not really – April Ghoul!

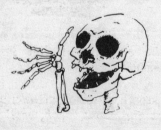

A salesman rang the doorbell of a house and when the door opened he sprinkled dust along the path and into the hall. 'What's this?' asked the surprised woman of the house. 'It's ghost dust,' said the salesman. 'If you sprinkle it on the ground you won't suffer from ghosts.' 'But we don't have ghosts,' protested the woman. 'You see,' the salesman beamed; 'it works!'

More booo-ks from the ghost library:

Spooky Voices by Mona Lott
The Ghost in the Dungeon by Howey Wails
The Lady Vanishes by Peter Out

'I used to be a werewolf, but I'm all right nowoooooooooooo!'

How do you stop a werewolf attacking you?
Throw a stick and shout, 'fetch, boy!'

A doctor lived next door to one of his most awkward patients. The patient made a real nuisance of himself all the time. If he didn't feel well during the day he'd run and bang on the doctor's door, shouting: 'Doctor, doctor, can you give me something for a headache?' And if he didn't feel well during the night, he'd bang on the wall and shout: 'Doctor, doctor, can you give me something for a stomach pain?'

At last, after many years, the patient died. A few days later, the doctor died as well, and by an amazing coincidence they were buried side by side in the churchyard. It was quiet and still that night, and the church clock struck 12. Suddenly the doctor heard a ghostly banging on the side of his cold, dark coffin. 'Doctor, doctor,' said a spooky voice, 'can you give me something for worms?'

Two kids were looking at a mummy on display in the British museum. '1000 BC,' one of them read aloud, looking at the sign on the case. 'What does that mean?' 'I expect it's the number of the car that ran him over,' said the other.

Petrifying poltergeists in the parlour

Why is the graveyard such a noisy place?
Because of all the coffin.

What kind of horse would a headless horseman ride?
A nightmare.

What do ghosts do every night at 11 o'clock?
Take a coffin break.

What jewels do ghosts wear?
Tomb stones.

If you want to hunt ghosts, what is the best way to keep fit?
Exorcise yourself.

What is a ghost's final drink?
His bier.

What do you get if you cross a ghost with a potato?
A spook-tater.

What is a ghost's favourite dessert?
Boo-berry pie with I-scream.

MOTHER GHOST TO SON: How many times do I have
to tell you — spook when you are spooken to.

FIRST GHOST: I saw *The Phantom of the Opera* on
television last night.
SECOND GHOST: Was it frightening?
FIRST GHOST: Yes, it half scared the life into me!

Why did the ghost go to the party?
To have a wail of a time.

Why do they put fences around graveyards?
Because people are dying to get in.

What would you call a ghost shepherdess?
Little Boo Peep.

Why did the ghost jump when his mother-in-law called?
Because he did not ex-spectre.

What did the ghost buy his wife for Christmas?
A see-through nightie.

What do you call ghosts on mountains?
High spirits.

What is an American ghost's favourite dessert?
Boo-berry pie.

What do you call the flying ghost of a sailor?
A sea ghoul.

Who teaches young ghosts?
A ghoulmaster.

What does a ghost enjoy?
Being shrouded in mystery.

Why did the skeleton stop going to parties?
He got tired of people hanging their hats and coats on him.

What frozen food company is run by ghouls?
Fiendus Foods.

What do you call two drunk ghosts?
Methylated spirits.

What do ghost busters write in?
Exorcise books.

Where do Spanish ghosts go on holiday?
The ghosta brava.

Where do American ghosts go for their holidays?
Boo York.

What is a young ghost's favourite TV programme?
Boo Peter.

What sort of eyes do ghosts have?
Terror-ize.

Where do ghosts go for their holidays?
Wails.

Why did the ghost go to Africa?
He wanted to become a big game haunter.

What do you call a phantom chicken?
A poultry-geist.

What do you call a failed phantom?
A paltry-geist.

What do you call a Polish phantom?
A Pole-tergeist.

What do you call a ghost who is a candidate in a General Election?
A poll-tergeist.

What do you call a hairy beast in a river?
A weir-wolf.

What do you call a hairy beast that no longer exists?
A were-wolf.

A hungry rabbit walked into a country pub and hopped on to the counter. 'Have you got anything to eat?' he asked the surprised landlord. 'As a matter of fact, we do have a new line in toasties,' the man replied. 'But I don't usually serve rabbits.' 'Oh please,' begged the rabbit, 'I'm absolutely starving.'

The landlord agreed, and the rabbit ordered an orange juice and a toastie. 'What sort of toastie would you like? We've got cheese toasties, ham toasties, chicken toasties, mushroom toasties, tomato toasties, baked bean toasties . . .' The rabbit ordered a tomato toastie and when it came he devoured it in seconds. Then he ordered a cheese toastie and a mushroom toastie as well. He gobbled these up, too, and ordered a baked bean toastie and a chicken one.

'You'll burst,' joked the landlord, but the rabbit finished them all off, paid his bill and left. Later that day the landlord opened the bar again, and into the room hopped the ghost of the rabbit. It jumped up on to the counter and stared at the landlord with its little red eyes. 'What happened?' asked the landlord. 'Were you run over by a car? Did a fox get you?' 'No,' sighed the rabbit ghost mournfully; 'I died of mixin' ma toasties.'

Frightening phantoms in the front room

What do ghosts call their navy?
The ghost guard.

What do you flatten a ghost with?
A spirit level.

What did the barman say when the ghost ordered
a gin and tonic?
'Sorry, we don't serve spirits.'

Which ghost has the best hearing?
The eeriest.

Why did the ghost teacher tell off the ghost pupil?
Because he kept making a ghoul of himself.

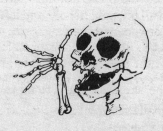

What would you do if you found that your bedroom
was haunted?
Find another bedroom.

How do ghosts pass through a locked door?
With a skeleton key.

Why didn't the skeleton want to go to school?
Because his heart wasn't in it.

What's a skeleton?
Bones with the people scraped off.

Which stall did the skeletons run at the graveyard
fête?
The rattle.

What do you call a skeleton that never does any
work?
Lazy bones.

Which musical instrument does a skeleton play?
A trom-bone.

What is a skeleton's favourite pop group?
Boney M.

What do you get if you cross a ghost with a boy scout?
A ghost that scares old ladies across the street.

How would you describe a punk ghost?
A real cool ghoul.

How do ghosts repair their clothes?
They use invisible mending.

How do you make a skeleton laugh?
Tickle his funny bone.

What do you get if you cross a ghost with a spider?
A creepy crawlie?

Why do skeletons hate winter?
Because the cold goes right through them.

What is the definition of noise?
Two skeletons break-dancing on a tin roof.

How do you know when a skeleton is upset?
He gets rattled.

What is a skeleton's favourite vegetable?
Marrow.

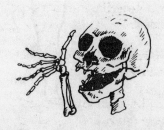

How do skeletons communicate with each other?
They use the tele-bone.

Did you hear about the lady ghost who did the can-can?
Ooooo-la-la.

What did the ghostly parrot say?
'Oooooo's a pretty boy then?'

What is the ghosts' favourite song?
'Ooooo's that Knocking at My Door?

What is the ghosts' favourite TV programme?
Ooooo Do You Do?

Why did the mother ghost take her child to the doctor?
Because it had ooooping cough.

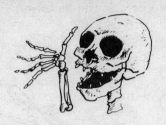

What do you call a hairy beast that's lost?
A where-wolf.

What happens if you cross a werewolf with a sheep?
You have to get a new sheep.

What do you get if you cross a werewolf with a flower?
I don't know, but I wouldn't recommend smelling it.

On which side does a werewolf have the most hair?
On the outside.

What is fearsome, hairy, and drinks from the wrong side of a glass?
A werewolf with hiccups.

How does a ghost do the housework?
With the ooooooo-ver.

Which ghost is an expert on bringing up children?
Dr Spook.

Why was the ghost arrested?
Because it was haunting without a licence.

'May I haunt your castle?' asked the polite ghost?
'Certainly,' answered his Lordship. 'Be my ghost.'

What do ghosts eat for breakfast?
Shrouded wheat.

What day do ghosts like best?
April Ghouls' Day.

What do you get if you cross a chicken with a ghost?
A peck-a-boo.

What do you find in an elephant's graveyard?
Elephantoms.

What did the ghost sentry call out to the intruder?
'Halt! Who ghosts there?'

What do spirits eat for breakfast?
Ghost toasties with boo-berries and evaporated milk.

Did you hear about the car that juddered to a halt
as soon as a ghost appeared?
It had a nervous breakdown.

In the middle of the night a man staying in a
haunted house came across a ghost in the corridor.
The ghost said: 'I have been walking these corridors
for more than 300 years.' 'Oh good,' said the man;
'in that case you can tell me the way to the toilet.'

How do young ghosts prefer their eggs?
Terror-fried.

Did you hear about the ghost rooster?
He woke everyone up with his spook-a-doodle-doos.

What do you call the ghost of a prehistoric bird?
A terror-dactyl.

Why are young ghosts at their noisiest in July and August?
Because they're on their howly-days.

What do ghosts write with?
Phantom pens.

When do banshees howl?
On Moanday night.

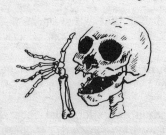

FIRST SOCIETY GHOST: What do you think of the new season's shrouds?
SECOND SOCIETY GHOST: I wouldn't be seen dead in them.

Hair-raising horrors in the hallway

A little girl was taken to her first seance. The medium asked: 'Is there anyone you would like to talk to?' 'Yes,' said the little girl. 'My grandmother.'

The medium closed her eyes for a minute. Then all of a sudden a voice spoke. 'Hello, my dear. This is your grandma speaking from heaven . . .' 'Hello grandma,' answered the girl. 'How come you're in heaven? You haven't even died yet!'

FIRST GHOST: That spook over there must have been a good driver when he was alive.
SECOND GHOST: How do you know that?
FIRST GHOST: He's just asked to be fitted with wing mirrors.

What goes 'Boo boo bang?'
A ghost in a minefield.

When does a ghost become two ghosts?
When he is beside himself.

What's green, has six legs and kills people by jumping on them from trees?
The phantom snooker table.

Why was the ghost policeman surprised when his girlfriend was arrested?
He didn't suspectre.

FIRST GHOSTBUSTER: What's that strange knocking noise? It must be a ghost.
SECOND GHOSTBUSTER: No, it's my knees.

Where do ghosts study?
At ghoul-lege.

Who said 'Shiver me timbers!' on the ghost ship?
The skeleton crew.

What job did the lady ghost have on the jumbo jet?
Air ghostess.

Where do ghouls and phantoms travel?
From ghost to ghost.

Did you hear about the stupid ghost?
He climbed over walls.

Why shouldn't you grab a werewolf by its tail?
It might be the werewolf's tail, but it could be your end.

Why are werewolves regarded as quick-witted?
Because they always give snappy answers.

Why did Mr and Mrs Werewolf call their son 'Camera'?
Because he was always snapping.

What's the difference between a werewolf and a flea?
A werewolf can have fleas but a flea cannot have werewolves.

What do you call a hairy beast with clothes on?
A wear-wolf.

Why did Dracula go to Olympia?
To see the Hearse of the Year Show.

What do ghosts put on their roast beef?
Grave-y.

What is the best thing to do if a ghost comes in through your front door?
Run out of the back door.

Did you hear about Romeo ghost meeting Juliet ghost?
It was love at first fright.

Why did the skeleton go to the party?
To have a rattling good time.

Why did the ghost's shroud fall down?
Because he had no visible means of support.

Why are ghosts always poor?
Because a ghoul and his money are soon parted.

What do you call a skeleton in a kilt?
Bony Prince Charlie.

How do ghosts like their drinks in summer?
Ice ghoul.

Where are ghosts when the lights go out?
In the dark.

Why did the one-handed skeleton cross the road?
To get to the second-hand shop.

Where would a Red Indian's ghost live?
In a creepy tepee.

FIRST GHOST: You give me eerie ache.
SECOND GHOST: Sorry I spook.

What do ghosts like about riding horses?
Ghoulloping.

Why are ghosts invisible?
They wear see-through clothes.

What is the name of the ghost's favourite pub?
The Horse and Gloom.

What do short-sighted ghosts wear?
Spook-tacles.

What walks through walls, saying 'Boo' very quietly?
A nervous ghost.

What trembles and says 'Oob'?
A nervous ghost walking through a wall backwards.

What do you call a play that's acted by ghosts?
A phantomime.

What do ghosts eat for breakfast?
Dreaded wheat

What do ghosts eat for lunch?
Ghoul-ash.

What do ghosts eat for supper?
Spook-etti.

How do worried ghosts look?
Grave.

Why are ghosts bad at telling lies?
Because you can see right through them.

What did the skeleton say to his girlfriend?
'I love every bone in your body.'

What did one ghost say to another?
'I'm sorry, but I just don't believe in people.'

Baleful banshees in the bedroom

Did you hear about the midget ghost?
He's too small to use a sheet — he has to wear a pillow case instead.

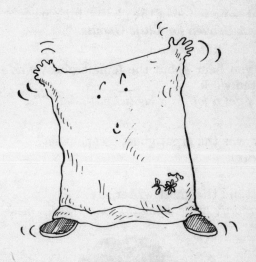

FIRST GHOST MOTHER: I can't control my daughter.
SECOND GHOST MOTHER: Why's that?
FIRST GHOST MOTHER: She's a very spirited girl!

What kind of make-up do female ghosts use?
Vanishing cream.

What song is top of the ghosts' hit parade?
Thank Heaven for Little Ghouls.

Did you hear about the female ghost who's just
started work?
She's got a job as a bootician!

Who was the great ghost escapologist?
Boodini.

What did the ghost writer say?
'I can only write when the spirit moves me.'

What did the old skeleton complain of?
Aching bones.

Why did the ghost look in the mirror?
To make sure he still wasn't there!

What country has the most ghosts?
Ghosta Rica.

What do you call it when a ghost makes a mistake?
A boo-boo.

What is a ghost's favourite TV programme?
Horror-nation Street.

What is a ghost's favourite day of the week?
Moanday.

Why didn't the skeleton want to go to school?
Because his heart wasn't in it.

What phantom was a famous painter?
Vincent van Ghost.

What do you call a TV show that stars ghosts and phantoms?
A spook-tacular.

What's a skeleton?
Bones with the people scraped off.

Why did the ghosts hold a seance?
To try to contact the living.

At the ghosts' school, which song is sung each day at morning assembly?
Ghoul Britannia.

The ghost teacher was showing her class how to walk through walls. 'Now did you all understand that?' she asked. 'If not, I'll just go through it again . . .'

Where do space ghosts live?
In far distant terror-tory.

Why did the ghost visit Russell Grant?
Because he wanted to see his horrorscope.

Which is the ghosts' favourite stretch of water?
Lake Eerie.

What do you do if you see a skeleton running across the road?
Jump out of your skin and join him.

What did the policeman say when he met the three-headed ghost?
' 'Ello, 'ello, 'ello.'

Where do you find ghost snails?
On the end of ghosts' fingers.

Where do ghosts like to swim?
In the Dead Sea.

What is the ghosts' favourite Wild West town?
Tombstone.

What's a ghost's favourite fairground ride?
The Roller Ghoster.

Why wouldn't the skeleton jump off the cliff?
Because he had no guts.

What did the little boy say when he saw the ghost
of Charles I?
'You must be off your head!'

What's a ghost's favourite book?
Ghoulliver's Travels.

How do English ghosts go abroad?
By British Scareways.

What did the ghost call his mother and father?
His transparents.

THE ROLLER GHOSTER

FIRST BOY: I met a ghost last night.
SECOND BOY: What did it say?
FIRST BOY: I don't know, I can't speak dead languages.

If you tipped a can of food over a ghoul, what would you get?
Beans on ghost.

Did you hear about the famous ghost politician?
He became Spooker of the House of Commons.

Why are old ghosts boring?
Because they're groan-ups.

What are the posh ghost's hobbies?
Haunting, shooting and fishing.

Which stall did the skeletons run at the graveyard fête?
The rattle.

What did one hippie ghost say to the other hippie ghost?
'Real ghoul, man.'

Where do ghosts live?
In dread-sitters.

What do you call an old and foolish vampire?
A silly old sucker.

What relation is Dracula to Frankenstein?
They are blood brothers.

What is Dracula's favourite drink?
A Bloody Mary.

What is Dracula's motto?
The morgue the merrier.

Why did the vampire fly over the mountain?
Because he couldn't fly under it.

Other great reads from *Red Fox*

Further Red Fox titles that you might enjoy reading are listed on the following pages. They are available in bookshops or they can be ordered directly from us.

If you would like to order books, please send this form and the money due to:

ARROW BOOKS, BOOKSERVICE BY POST, PO BOX 29, DOUGLAS, ISLE OF MAN, BRITISH ISLES. Please enclose a cheque or postal order made out to Arrow Books Ltd for the amount due, plus 22p per book for postage and packing, both for orders within the UK and for overseas orders.

NAME _____

ADDRESS _____

_____

Please print clearly.

Whilst every effort is made to keep prices low, it is sometimes necessary to increase cover prices at short notice. If you are ordering books by post, to save delay it is advisable to phone to confirm the correct price. The number to ring is THE SALES DEPARTMENT 071 (if outside London) 973 9700.

Other great reads from Red Fox

AMAZING ORIGAMI FOR CHILDREN
Steve and Megumi Biddle

Origami is an exciting and easy way to make toys, decorations and all kinds of useful things from folded paper.

Use leftover gift paper to make a party hat and a fancy box. Or create a colourful lorry, a pretty rose and a zoo full of origami animals. There are over 50 fun projects in Amazing Origami.

Following Steve and Megumi's step-by-step instructions and clear drawings, you'll amaze your friends and family with your magical paper creations.

ISBN 0 09 9661802   £4.99

MAGICAL STRING   Steve and Megumi Biddle

With only a loop of string you can make all kinds of shapes, puzzles and games. Steve and Megumi Biddle provide all the instructions and diagrams that are needed to create their amazing string magic in another of their inventive and absorbing books.

ISBN 0 09 964470 3   £2.50

Other great reads from **Red Fox**

Discover the wide range of exciting activity books from Red Fox

THE PAINT AND PRINT FUN BOOK
Steve and Megumi Biddle

Would you like to make a glittering bird? A colourful tiger? A stained-glass window? Or an old treasure map? Well, all you need are ordinary materials like vegetables, tinfoil, paper doilies, even your own fingers to make all kinds of amazing things—without too much mess.

Follow Steve and Megumi's step-by-step instructions and clear diagrams and you can make all kinds of professional designs—to hang on your wall or give to your friends.

ISBN 0 09 9644606   £2.50

CRAZY KITES   Peter Eldin

This book is a terrific introduction to the art of flying kites. There are lots of easy-to-assemble, different kites to make, from the basic flat kite to the Chinese dragon and the book also gives you clear instructions on launching, flying and landing. Kite flying is fun. Help yourself to a soaring good time.

ISBN 0 09 964550 5   £2.50

Other great reads ✒ *from* **Red Fox**

CRAZY PRESENTS   Juliet Bawden

Would you like to make: Pebble paper weights? Green tomato chutney? Scented hand cream? Patchwork clowns? Leather ties?

By following the step-by-step instructions in this book you can make a huge variety of gifts—from rattles for the very young to footwarmers for the very old. Some cost a few pence, others a little more but all are extra special presents.

ISBN 0 09 967080 1   £2.50

CRAZY PAPER   Eric Kenneway

Origami—the Japanese art of paper folding—is easy and fun to do. You can make boats that float, wriggling snakes, tumbling acrobats, jumping frogs and many more fantastic creatures.

There are easy to follow instructions and clear diagrams in this classic guide used by Japanese schoolchildren.

ISBN 0 09 951380 3   £1.95